CLASSICAL FAVORITES

CONTENTS

ISBN 978-0-634-06825-6

Hal•LEONARD®
CORPORATION
7777 W. BLUEMOUND RD. P.O. BOX 13819 MILWAUKEE, WI 53213

For all works contained herein:
Unauthorized copying, arranging, adapting, recording or public performance is an infringement of copyright.
Infringers are liable under the law.

Visit Hal Leonard Online at
www.halleonard.com

EINE KLEINE NACHTMUSIK

By W.A. MOZART

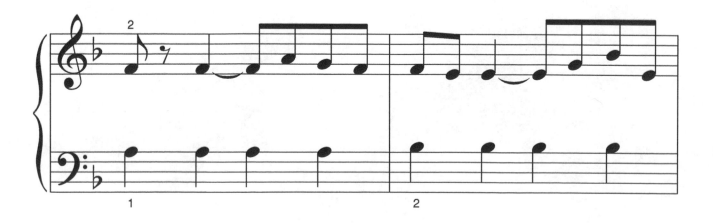

Copyright © 2004 by HAL LEONARD CORPORATION
International Copyright Secured   All Rights Reserved

4

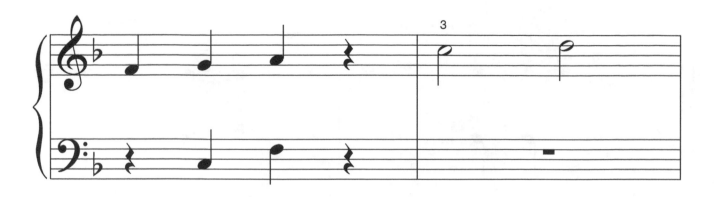

To Coda ⊕

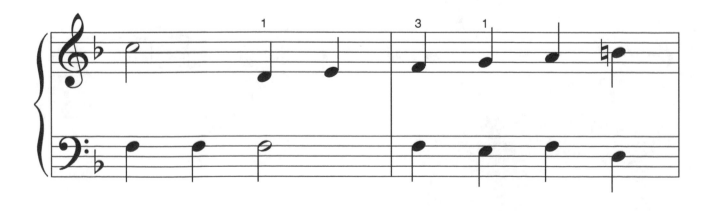

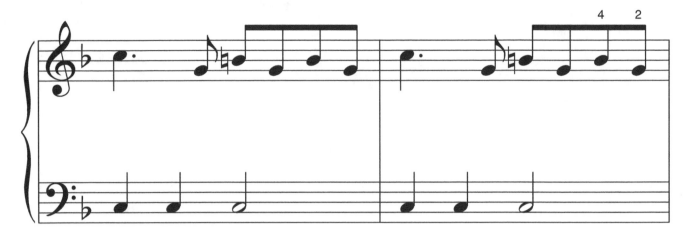

D.C. al Coda

CODA

FÜR ELISE

By LUDWIG VAN BEETHOVEN

Flowing

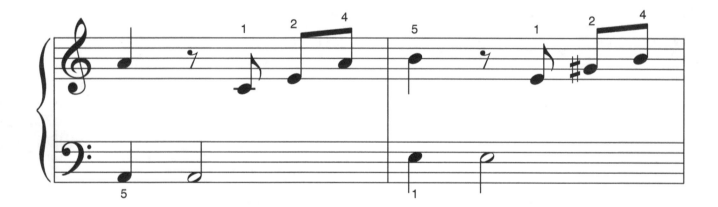

Copyright © 2004 by HAL LEONARD CORPORATION
International Copyright Secured   All Rights Reserved

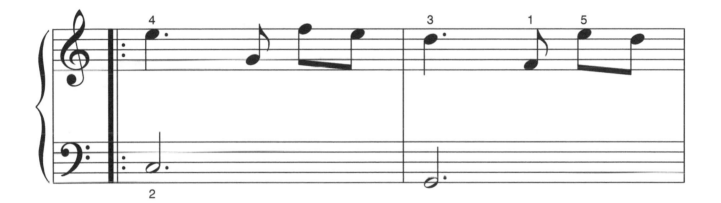

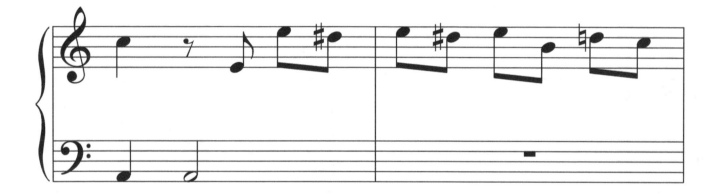

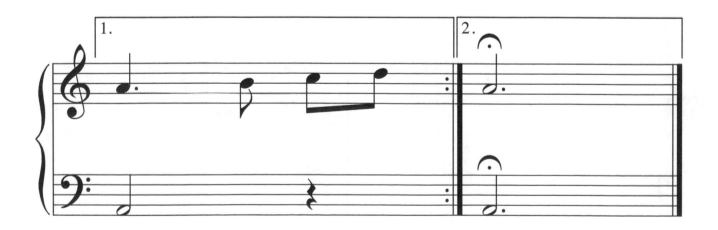

POMP AND CIRCUMSTANCE

Words by ARTHUR BENSON
Music by EDWARD ELGAR

Slowly (♩ = 1 beat)

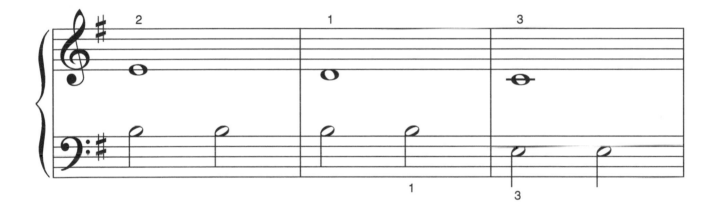

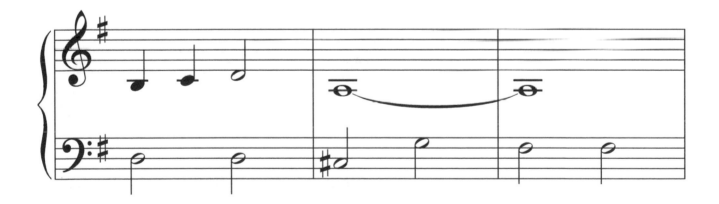

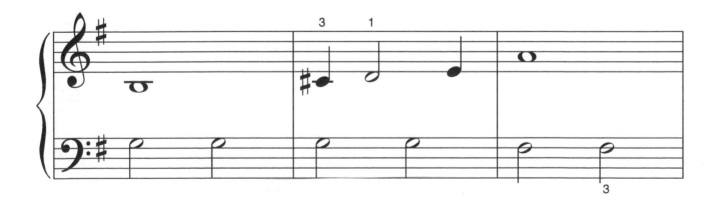

Copyright © 2004 by HAL LEONARD CORPORATION
International Copyright Secured   All Rights Reserved

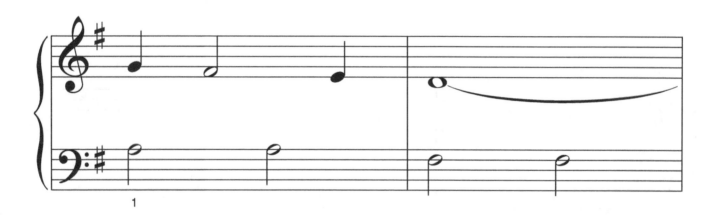

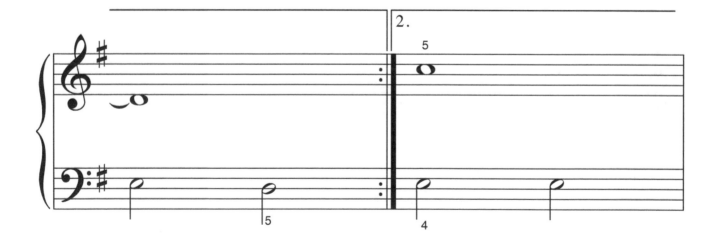

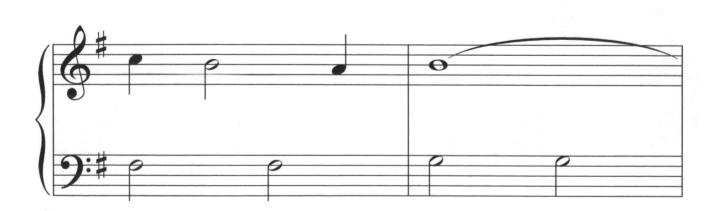

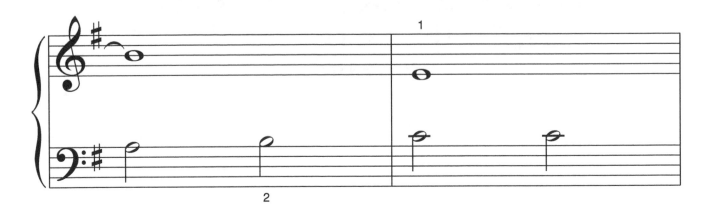

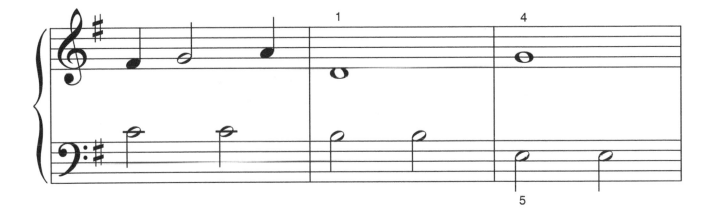

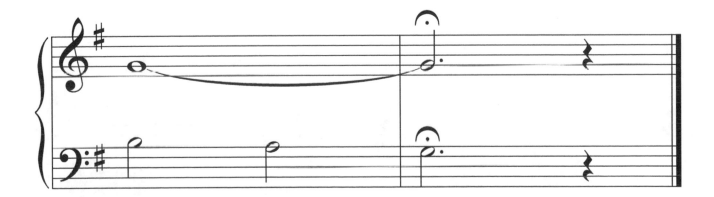

IN THE HALL OF THE MOUNTAIN KING

from PEER GYNT

By EDVARD GRIEG

Slow March

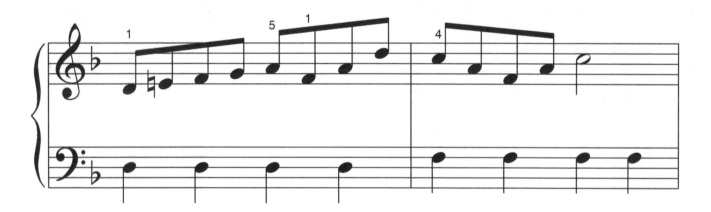

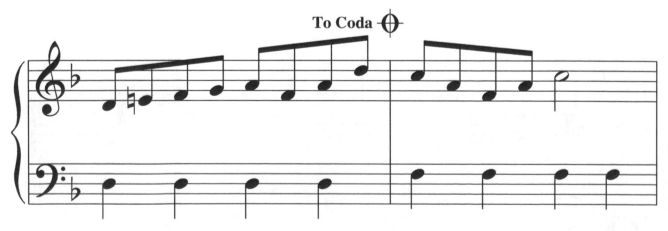

Copyright © 2004 by HAL LEONARD CORPORATION
International Copyright Secured All Rights Reserved

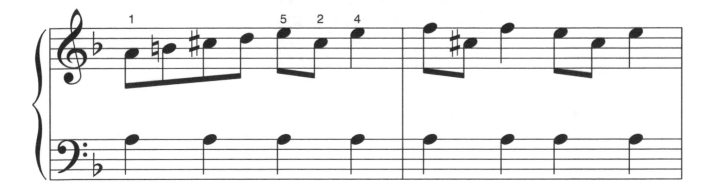

D.C. al Coda

CODA

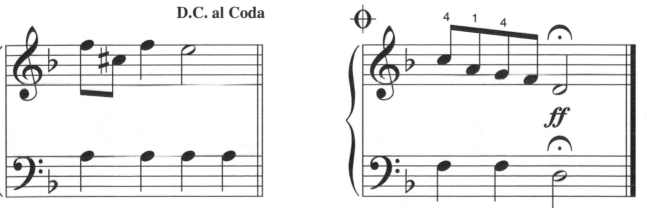

MARCH
from THE NUTCRACKER

By PYOTR IL'YICH TCHAIKOVSKY

Moderately

Copyright © 2004 by HAL LEONARD CORPORATION
International Copyright Secured   All Rights Reserved

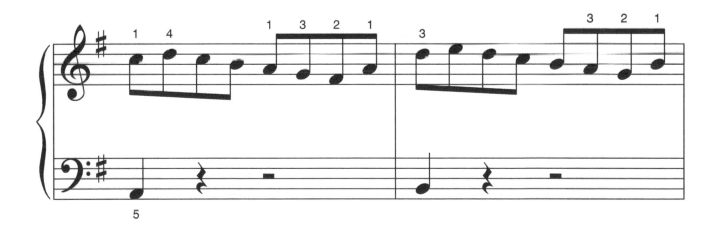

MINUET IN G MAJOR

By JOHANN SEBASTIAN BACH

Moderately

Copyright © 2004 by HAL LEONARD CORPORATION
International Copyright Secured   All Rights Reserved

ODE TO JOY

from SYMPHONY NO. 9 IN D MINOR, FOURTH MOVEMENT CHORAL THEME

Words by HENRY VAN DYKE
Music by LUDWIG VAN BEETHOVEN

With spirit

Copyright © 2004 by HAL LEONARD CORPORATION
International Copyright Secured   All Rights Reserved

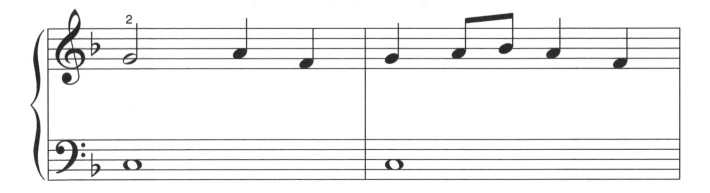

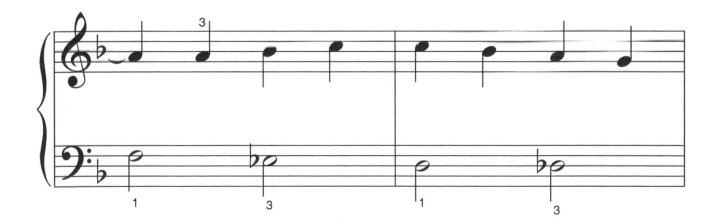

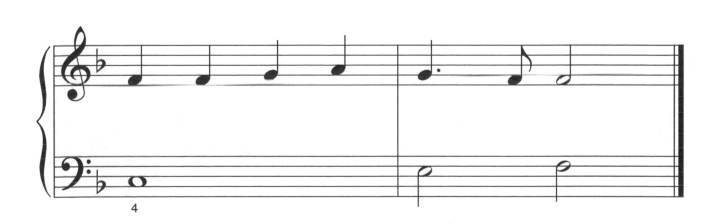

PACHELBEL'S CANON

By JOHANN PACHELBEL

Slowly

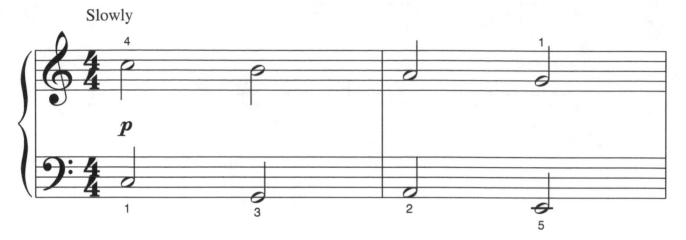

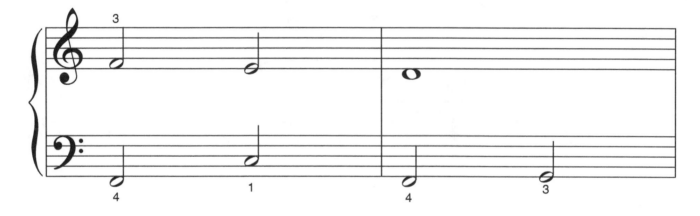

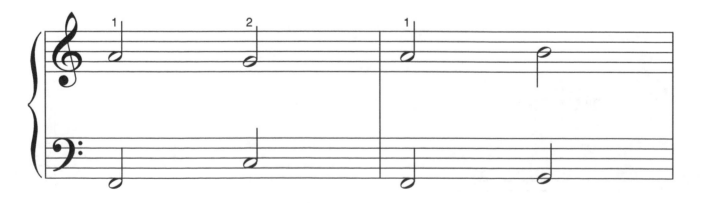

Copyright © 2004 by HAL LEONARD CORPORATION
Intenational Copyright Secured   All Rights Reserved

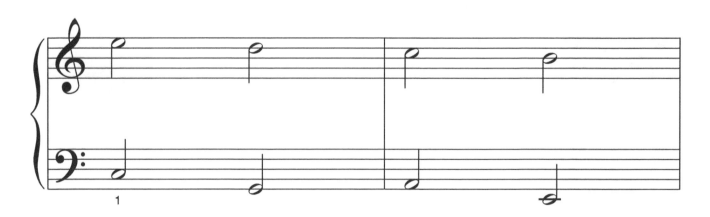

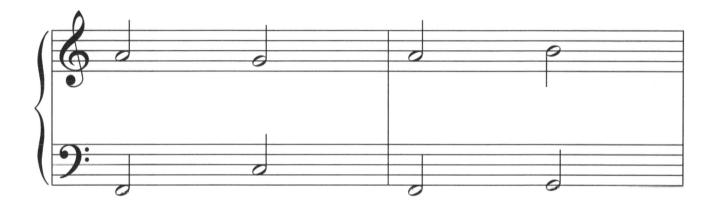

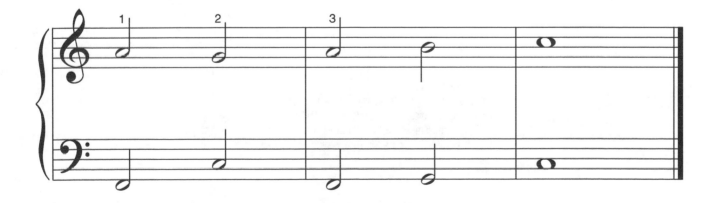

Big Fun with Big-Note Piano Books!

These songbooks feature exciting easy arrangements for beginning piano students.

Best of Adele
Now even beginners can play their favorite Adele tunes! This book features big-note arrangements of 10 top songs: Chasing Pavements • Daydreamer • Hometown Glory • Lovesong • Make You Feel My Love • One and Only • Rolling in the Deep • Set Fire to the Rain • Someone like You • Turning Tables.
00308601 .... $14.99

Beatles' Best
27 classics for beginners to enjoy, including: Can't Buy Me Love • Eleanor Rigby • Hey Jude • Michelle • Here, There and Everywhere • When I'm Sixty-Four • Yesterday • and more.
00222561 .... $14.99

The Best Songs Ever
70 favorites, featuring: Body and Soul • Crazy • Edelweiss • Fly Me to the Moon • Georgia on My Mind • Imagine • The Lady Is a Tramp • Memory • A String of Pearls • Tears in Heaven • Unforgettable • You Are So Beautiful • and more.
00310425 .... $19.95

Children's Favorite Movie Songs
arranged by Phillip Keveren
16 favorites from films, including: The Bare Necessities • Beauty and the Beast • Can You Feel the Love Tonight • Do-Re-Mi • The Rainbow Connection • Tomorrow • Zip-A-Dee-Doo-Dah • and more.
00310838 .... $12.99

Classical Music's Greatest Hits
24 beloved classical pieces, including: Air on the G String • Ave Maria • By the Beautiful Blue Danube • Canon in D • Eine Kleine Nachtmusik • Für Elise • Ode to Joy • Romeo and Juliet • Waltz of the Flowers • more.
00310475 .... $12.99

Disney Big-Note Collection
Over 40 Disney favorites, including: Circle of Life • Colors of the Wind • Hakuna Matata • It's a Small World • Under the Sea • A Whole New World • Winnie the Pooh • Zip-A-Dee-Doo-Dah • and more.
00316056 .... $19.99

Essential Classical
22 simplified piano pieces from top composers, including: Ave Maria (Schubert) • Blue Danube Waltz (Strauss) • Für Elise (Beethoven) • Jesu, Joy of Man's Desiring (Bach) • Morning (Grieg) • Pomp and Circumstance (Elgar) • and many more.
00311205 .... $10.99

Favorite Children's Songs
arranged by Bill Boyd
29 easy arrangements of songs to play and sing with children: Peter Cottontail • I Whistle a Happy Tune • It's a Small World • On the Good Ship Lollipop • The Rainbow Connection • and more!
00240251 .... $12.99

Frozen
9 songs from this hit Disney film, plus full-color illustrations from the movie. Songs include the standout single "Let It Go", plus: Do You Want to Build a Snowman? • For the First Time in Forever • Reindeer(s) Are Better Than People • and more.
00126105 .... $12.99

Happy Birthday to You and Other Great Songs for Big-Note Piano
16 essential favorites, including: Chitty Chitty Bang Bang • Good Night • Happy Birthday to You • Heart and Soul • Over the Rainbow • Sing • This Land Is Your Land • and more.
00119636 .... $9.99

Elton John – Greatest Hits
20 of his biggest hits, including: Bennie and the Jets • Candle in the Wind • Crocodile Rock • Rocket Man • Tiny Dancer • Your Song • and more.
00221832 .... $14.99

Les Misérables
14 favorites from the Broadway sensation arranged for beginning pianists. Titles include: At the End of the Day • Bring Him Home • Castle on a Cloud • I Dreamed a Dream • In My Life • On My Own • Who Am I? • and more.
00221812 .... $15.99

The Phantom of the Opera
9 songs from the Broadway spectacular, including: All I Ask of You • Angel of Music • Masquerade • The Music of the Night • The Phantom of the Opera • The Point of No Return • Prima Donna • Think of Me • Wishing You Were Somehow Here Again.
00110006 .... $14.99

Pride & Prejudice
Music from the Motion Picture Soundtrack
12 piano pieces from the 2006 Oscar-nominated film: Another Dance • Darcy's Letter • Georgiana • Leaving Netherfield • Liz on Top of the World • Meryton Townhall • The Secret Life of Daydreams • Stars and Butterflies • and more.
00316125 .... $12.99

The Sound of Music
arranged by Phillip Keveren
9 favorites: Climb Ev'ry Mountain • Do-Re-Mi • Edelweiss • The Lonely Goatherd • Maria • My Favorite Things • Sixteen Going on Seventeen • So Long, Farewell • The Sound of Music.
00316057 .... $10.99

Best of Taylor Swift
A dozen top tunes from this crossover sensation: Fearless • Fifteen • Hey Stephen • Love Story • Our Song • Picture to Burn • Teardrops on My Guitar • White Horse • You Belong with Me • and more.
00307143 .... $12.99

Worship Favorites
20 powerful songs: Above All • Come, Now Is the Time to Worship • I Could Sing of Your Love Forever • More Precious Than Silver • Open the Eyes of My Heart • Shout to the Lord • and more.
00311207 .... $12.99

HAL•LEONARD®

Prices, contents, and availability subject to change without notice. Disney Characters and Artwork TM & © 2019 Disney.